P9-ASH-808

SPORTS' GREATEST OF ALL TIME

BASKETBALL'S G.O.A.T.

MICHAEL JORDAN, LEBRON JAMES, AND MORE

JOE LEVIT

Lerner Publications ◆ Minneapolis

Copyright © 2020 by Lerner Publishing Group, Inc.

All rights reserved. International copyright secured. No part of this book may be reproduced, stored in a retrieval system, or transmitted in any form or by any means—electronic, mechanical, photocopying, recording, or otherwise—without the prior written permission of Lerner Publishing Group, Inc., except for the inclusion of brief quotations in an acknowledged review.

Lerner Publications Company
A division of Lerner Publishing Group, Inc.
241 First Avenue North
Minneapolis, MN 55401 USA

For reading levels and more information, look up this title at www.lernerbooks.com.

Main body text set in Aptifer Sans LT Pro.
Typeface provided by Linotype AG.

Library of Congress Cataloging-in-Publication Data

Names: Levit, Joseph, author.
Title: Basketball's G.O.A.T. : Michael Jordan, LeBron James, and more / Joe Levit.
Other titles: Basketball's GOAT | Basketball's greatest of all time
Description: Minneapolis : Lerner Publications, 2020. | Series: Sports' greatest of all time | Includes bibliographical references and index. | Audience: Age 7–11. | Audience: Grade 4 to 6.
Identifiers: LCCN 2018044204 (print) | LCCN 2018044976 (ebook) | ISBN 9781541556355 (eb pdf) | ISBN 9781541556010 (lb : alk. paper)
Subjects: LCSH: Basketball players—United States—Biography—Juvenile literature.
Classification: LCC GV884.A1 (ebook) | LCC GV884.A1 L48 2020 (print) | DDC 796.323092/2 [B] —dc23

LC record available at https://lccn.loc.gov/2018044204

Manufactured in the United States of America
1-46057-43473-2/13/2019

CONTENTS

TIP-OFF!

Each season, National Basketball Association (NBA) fans talk about who deserves the Most Valuable Player (MVP) Award. The prize goes to the best player in the league that season. But have you ever thought about the best players in league history? That's a harder thing to determine. How do you compare players from different eras?

The NBA formed in 1949. From 1967 to 1976, a pro league

FACTS AT A GLANCE

HAKEEM OLAJUWON blocked 3,830 shots in his career, more than any other player in NBA history did.

LARRY BIRD won the regular-season MVP three years in a row from 1984 to 1986. He led the Boston Celtics to victory in the NBA Finals in two of those seasons.

DIANA TAURASI is the WNBA's all-time leader in points with 8,549. Her 1,835 assists are fourth all-time.

WILT CHAMBERLAIN scored 100 points in a single game, the most in NBA history.

called the American Basketball Association (ABA) competed with the NBA. Unlike the NBA, the ABA allowed three-point shots. Three-pointers added excitement to ABA games. The two leagues became one in 1976. But the NBA didn't adopt the three-point shot until 1979. The rule changed the year Larry Bird joined the league. He took advantage of it by hitting 649 three-point shots in his career.

Women's basketball became an Olympic Games sport in 1976. In 1997, NBA owners started the Women's National Basketball Association (WNBA). The pro league started with eight teams and grew to 12 teams by 2010. The WNBA's success helped great women players become stars in the United States.

Kim Perrot of the Houston Comets dribbles past a defender. The Comets won the first four WNBA championships.

The modern NBA has 30 teams spread around the United States and Canada.

The players in this book deserve to be called the G.O.A.T.—the greatest of all time. You may disagree with the order of the players. Your friends may rank the greatest basketball players differently too. Maybe you feel someone important has been left out. Remarkable athletes such as Kobe Bryant, Sheryl Swoopes, Oscar Robertson, Shaquille O'Neal, and Bill Russell missed the cut. It's okay to disagree. Thinking about great pro players and forming your own opinions about them is what this book is all about!

HAKEEM OLAJUWON

Hakeem Olajuwon led the Houston Rockets to two straight championships in 1994 and 1995. He was a nightmare for defenders to stop. Olajuwon is one of only four players in NBA history to record a quadruple-double. He did it in 1990 with 18 points, 16 rebounds, 11 blocked shots, and 10 assists in one game. His fast footwork

helped him fake out defenders near the basket. He turned one way before quickly spinning the other way for an open shot. The move, called the Dream Shake, was almost impossible to defend.

Olajuwon was just as good on defense. He was a two-time NBA Defensive Player of the Year. His 3,830 blocked shots are the most ever. He is ninth all-time with 2,162 steals, an amazing stat for a center. In the 1993–1994 season, his skills helped him become the first player to win the NBA MVP Award, the Finals MVP Award, and the Defensive Player of the Year honor in the same season.

HAKEEM OLAJUWON STATS

► He was All-NBA First Team six times.

► He won the NBA MVP Award for the 1993–1994 season.

► He won the NBA Finals MVP Award in 1993–1994 and 1994–1995.

► He was All-Defensive First Team five times.

► He is third all-time with 3.1 blocked shots

#9

MAYA MOORE

Maya Moore can do almost everything on a basketball court. She grabs rebounds and plays tough defense. She scores close to the basket and from long range. Her skills have made her one of the most successful basketball players ever. In 2010, Moore became the all-time leading scorer for the University of Connecticut Huskies. She also helped the team win two national championships during her college career.

Moore kept on winning after college. She and Team USA won gold medals at the Olympic Games in 2012 and 2016. Yet her greatest successes may have come in the WNBA as a member of the Minnesota Lynx. Moore helped her team reach the WNBA Finals six times in her first seven seasons. They won four championships during that time. Along the way, Moore became Minnesota's all-time leader in three-point baskets, steals, and blocked shots.

MAYA MOORE STATS

▶ She won the WNBA Rookie of the Year award in 2011.

▶ She won the WNBA MVP award in 2014.

▶ She was All-WNBA First Team five times.

▶ She won the 2013 WNBA Finals MVP award.

▶ She is seventh in WNBA history with an average of 18.4 points per game.

#8

LARRY BIRD

What set Larry Bird apart from many NBA players was his deep desire to win. Bird's passion made him a top-notch trash-talker. He tried to get inside the heads of his opponents. But he backed up his words with actions. Bird did everything well. He played tough defense. He finished the season in the top 10 in rebounds nine times. He was top 10 in steals three

times. Yet fans knew him best as an unstoppable scorer. He could shoot the ball with a lightning-fast flick of his wrist. And he was deadly accurate.

The Boston Celtics won three championships in Bird's 13-year career. The team's best season with Bird may have been 1985–1986. He helped the team win 67 of 82 games that year. Just six teams have ever won more games in a single season. The Celtics went on to defeat the Houston Rockets in the Finals.

LARRY BIRD STATS

▶ He was All-NBA First Team nine times.

▶ He won the NBA MVP Award three years in a row from 1984 to 1986.

▶ He won the NBA Finals MVP Award in 1983–1984 and 1985–1986.

▶ He finished in the top five in NBA MVP voting nine times.

▶ His 24.29 career points per game is 15th best in NBA history.

#7

TIM DUNCAN

Tim Duncan's nickname, the Big Fundamental, tells you all you need to know about him as a player. Duncan's footwork and other basic basketball skills were special. They helped him control the game on both offense and defense. He wasn't flashy. But his all-around skills helped make him a longtime NBA superstar. He was a consistent force for 19 seasons with the San Antonio Spurs. During

that time, he played a key part on some of the league's best teams.

Duncan teamed up with fellow superstar David Robinson to win the NBA title in 1999. Robinson retired in 2003, but Duncan and San Antonio kept winning. He helped the Spurs win four more championships. Duncan rarely made mistakes. He often jumped for a key block or sank a clutch shot. He usually came up with a big play just when his team needed it most.

TIM DUNCAN STATS

▶ He was All-NBA First Team 10 times.

▶ He was All-Defensive First Team eight times.

▶ He won the NBA MVP Award in 2001–2002 and 2002–2003.

▶ He won the NBA Finals MVP Award three times.

▶ He is sixth all-time in blocked shots with 3,020.

MAGIC JOHNSON

Earvin Johnson became Magic Johnson after a sportswriter saw him score 36 points in a high school game. The writer called him Magic, and the nickname stuck. Johnson led the Los Angeles Lakers in the 1980s. Fans loved his big smile and slick ball-handling skills. He was a guard, but he could play many positions well. His ability to move around the court came in handy during

his rookie season. Center Kareem Abdul-Jabbar missed Game 6 of the 1980 NBA Finals with an injured ankle. Johnson filled in at center and led the Lakers to victory over the Philadelphia 76ers.

Johnson's team reached the NBA Finals nine times with him in the lineup. They won the championship five of those seasons. Johnson always found the open man and delivered the ball to him. He is the top player all-time with 11.19 assists per game. John Stockton is a distant second at 10.51 assists per game.

MAGIC JOHNSON STATS

- ▶ He was All-NBA First Team nine times.

- ▶ He won the NBA MVP Award three times.

- ▶ He won the NBA Finals MVP Award three times.

- ▶ He ranks fifth all-time in assists with 10,141.

- ▶ He is the only player to win the NBA Finals MVP Award in his rookie season.

#5

DIANA TAURASI

Guards need to score from a long distance, and no one does that better than Diana Taurasi does. She wowed fans with her incredible shooting at the University of Connecticut. Her teams were some of the best in college basketball history. She led the Huskies to three straight championships from 2002 to 2004. Taurasi won the Naismith College Player of the Year award in 2003 and 2004.

After college, she brought her scoring power to the WNBA. The Phoenix Mercury won the WNBA Finals in 2007, 2009, and 2014 with Taurasi leading the way. No one can match her ability to put the ball in the basket. Taurasi is the WNBA's all-time leader in points with 8,549. She also holds the career record for three-point baskets made.

But scoring points isn't everything. Her teams win because she knows she can't do it alone. Taurasi's 1,835 assists are fourth most in league history.

DIANA TAURASI STATS

▶ She won the WNBA Rookie of the Year award in 2004.

▶ She won the WNBA MVP award in 2009.

▶ She was All-WNBA First Team 10 times.

▶ She won the WNBA Finals MVP award in 2009 and 2014.

▶ She holds the WNBA all-time points lead by more than 1,000 points.

WILT CHAMBERLAIN

Wilt Chamberlain was so skilled and worked so hard that he dominated the NBA in the 1960s and 1970s. Standing more than 7 feet (2.1 m) tall, he was a menace to opposing teams on both defense and offense. Chamberlain is the all-time leader in rebounds with 23,924. He also scored 30.07 points per game. That career average is second only to Michael Jordan's 30.12.

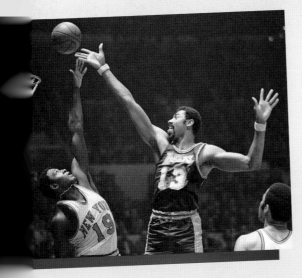

Chamberlain never seemed to tire. During his career, he played the most minutes per game in NBA history. In the 1961–1962 season, he averaged a whopping 48.5 minutes per game. Games lasted just 48 minutes, but Chamberlain topped that by playing in overtime.

Chamberlain was unstoppable that season for the Philadelphia Warriors. He averaged an amazing 50.4 points and 25.7 rebounds. On March 2, 1962, he scored 100 points in a game against the New York Knicks. That's still the most points ever scored in an NBA game.

WILT CHAMBERLAIN STATS

He was All-NBA First Team seven times.

He won the NBA MVP Award four times.

He won the NBA Finals MVP Award in 1971–1972.

His 22.9 rebounds per game is the best average in NBA history.

He led the NBA in scoring seven seasons

#3

KAREEM ABDUL-JABBAR

Kareem Abdul-Jabbar won three straight college basketball championships in the late 1960s. Then he continued to win in the NBA for 20 seasons. He won his first NBA title in 1971 with the Milwaukee Bucks. In 1975, the Bucks traded him to the Los Angeles Lakers. He went on to help Los Angeles win five championships.

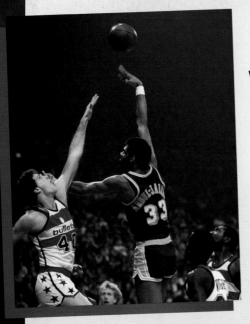

Abdul-Jabbar's famous skyhook shot was almost unstoppable. He would leap in the air with one shoulder facing his opponent. With his opposite hand, he'd launch a one-armed shot over the fingers of the defender. The ball would travel in a high arc toward the hoop. Then it would usually swish through the net for two points. Abdul-Jabbar made more than 50 percent of his shots in every season except his last. His 38,387 points are the most scored by any player in NBA history.

KAREEM ABDUL-JABBAR STATS

▶ He was All-NBA First Team ten times.

▶ He won the NBA MVP Award six times.

▶ He won the NBA Finals MVP Award in 1970–1971 and 1984–1985.

▶ He is in second place all-time with 1,560 games played.

▶ He was All-Defensive First Team five times.

MICHAEL JORDAN

Michael Jordan was perhaps the fiercest competitor to play in the NBA. He was known for taking the biggest shots in the biggest games—and he usually made them. He simply refused to lose. Fans loved Jordan's high-flying moves. He'd leap for an athletic dunk one moment and soar to block a taller player's shot the next. His stats were often spectacular. In 1987–1988, Jordan averaged 35 points,

5.5 rebounds, 5.9 assists, 3.2 steals, and 1.6 blocks per game. He scored the most points in the NBA and won the MVP and Defensive Player of the Year Awards.

A big part of what made Jordan so special was his defense. He ranks third all-time in steals with 2,514. Jordan's strong play at both ends of the court helped the Chicago Bulls win six NBA championships. They won the title three years in a row. Then, after a brief two-year retirement, Jordan returned to the NBA to help the Bulls win another three titles in a row.

MICHAEL JORDAN STATS

▶ He was All-NBA First Team 10 times.

▶ He won the NBA MVP Award five times.

▶ He won the NBA Finals MVP Award six times.

▶ He is fourth on the all-time list with 32,292 points scored.

▶ He was All-Defensive First Team nine times.

LEBRON JAMES

Los Angeles Lakers superstar LeBron James jumped straight from high school to the NBA. At the age of 23, he carried the Cleveland Cavaliers to the NBA Finals. Since then, he's led teams to the Finals eight more times, winning three titles.

James is one of the NBA's greatest scorers. He will soon pass legends such as Kobe Bryant, Wilt Chamberlain, and Michael Jordan on the all-time points list. James is also a fantastic defender. He can devastate the other team with a soul-sucking block or steal.

Perhaps his biggest feat was beating the Golden State Warriors in the 2016 NBA Finals. The Warriors had the best regular-season record in NBA history. They won 73 games and lost only nine. In the Finals, the Warriors led three games to one. But James fought back hard. He averaged 36 points per game while leading his team to three straight wins. James and the Cavaliers became the first team to win the NBA Finals after being down 3–1.

LEBRON JAMES STATS

► He has been All-NBA First Team 12 times.

► He has won the NBA MVP Award four times.

► He has won the NBA Finals MVP Award three times.

► His 27.2 points-per-game average is the fourth best ever.

► He has been All-Defensive First Team five times.

YOUR G.O.A.T.

IT'S YOUR TURN TO MAKE A G.O.A.T. LIST ABOUT PRO BASKETBALL. Start by doing research. Consider the rankings in this book. Then check out the Further Information section on page 31. Explore the books and websites to learn more about basketball players of the past and present.

You can search online for more information about great players too. Check with a librarian, who may have other resources for you. You might even try reaching out to NBA teams or players to see what they think.

Once you're ready, make your list of the greatest players of all time. Then ask people you know to make G.O.A.T. lists and compare them. Do you have players that no one else listed? Are you missing anybody that your friends think is important? Talk it over, and try to convince them that your list is the G.O.A.T.!

BASKETBALL FACTS

▶ Shaquille O'Neal made just one three-point shot during his 19-year NBA career. He sank 11,329 two-point baskets.

▶ During the 1987–1988 season, both the tallest player and the shortest player in NBA history played for the Washington Bullets. Manute Bol was 7 feet 7 inches (2.3 m) tall. Muggsy Bogues stood just 5 feet 3 inches (1.6 m).

▶ In 1991, the Cleveland Cavaliers beat the Miami Heat, 148–80. This 68-point margin of victory is the largest ever.

▶ Only four NBA players have ever accomplished a quadruple-double. No one has ever reached double digits in all five main stats categories in a single game.

▶ Only two players have averaged a triple-double for an entire season. Oscar Robertson averaged 30.8 points, 12.5 rebounds, and 11.4 assists per game in 1961–1962. Russell Westbrook averaged a triple-double twice, in 2016–2017 and 2017–2018.

GLOSSARY

All-Defensive First Team: one of the five best defensive players in the NBA based on votes by sports media members

All-NBA First Team: one of the five best overall players in the NBA based on votes by sports media members

All-WNBA First Team: one of the five best overall players in the WNBA based on votes by sports media members

assist: when a player passes the ball to another player who scores

blocked shot: when a defensive player touches the ball and causes a shot to miss the basket

center: a player positioned in the middle of the court near the basket

footwork: the position and movement of a player's feet

guard: a player positioned in the backcourt away from the basket

quadruple-double: when a player reaches double digits in four of the five main stats during a game. The five main stats are assists, blocked shots, points, rebounds, and steals.

rebound: when a player grabs a loose ball after a missed shot

steal: when a defender takes the ball from an offensive player without committing a foul

FURTHER INFORMATION

Jr. NBA
https://jr.nba.com/

Kramer, Sydelle. *Basketball's Greatest Players*. New York: Random House, 2015.

Monson, James. *Behind the Scenes Basketball*. Minneapolis: Lerner Publications, 2020.

NBA at 50: Top 50 Players
http://www.nba.com/history/nba-at-50/top-50-players

Savage, Jeff. *Basketball Super Stats*. Minneapolis: Lerner Publications, 2018.

WNBA.com
https://www.wnba.com/

INDEX

PHOTO ACKNOWLEDGMENTS

Image credits: conrado/Shutterstock.com, (throughout); Focus On Sport/
Contributor/Getty Images, pp. 4, 8, 12, 13 (top and bottom), 16, 17 (top and
bottom), 21 (bottom), 23 (top and bottom); DinoZ/Shutterstock.com, pp. 4,
28 (metal texture); Doug Pensinger/Staff/Getty Images, p. 6; Stacy Revere/
Contributor/Getty Images, p. 7; The Sporting News/Contributor/Getty Images,
p. 9 (top and bottom); Grant Halverson/Contributor/Getty Images, p. 10; Kevin C.
Cox/Getty Images, p. 11 (top); Tim Clayton-Corbis/Contributor/Getty Images, p. 11
(bottom); Tom Hauck/Staff/Getty Images, p. 14; Brian Bahr/Staff/Getty Images,
p. 15 (bottom); Paul Buck/Stringer/Getty Images, p. 15 (top); Christian Peterson/
Staff/Getty Images, pp. 18–19; Bettmann/Contributor/Getty Images, pp. 20, 21
(top); Stephen Dunn/Staff/Getty Images, p. 22; Jeff Haynes/Staff/Getty Images,
p. 24–25; Larry W. Smith/Pool/Getty Images, p. 26; Chris Trotman/Stringer/Getty
Images, p. 27 (top); Steve Dykes/Stringer/Getty Images, p. 27 (bottom); Sorapop
Udomsri/Shutterstock.com, p. 28 (basketball).

Cover: Robert Laberge/Getty Images; Jonathan Daniel/Allsport/Getty Images;
EFKS/Shutterstock.com.